T0198720

Unraveled Love

Poems by Heart

Rida Gulati

authorHOUSE®

AuthorHouse™
1663 Liberty Drive
Bloomington, IN 47403
www.authorhouse.com
Phone: 1 (800) 839-8640

Published by AuthorHouse 03/23/2018

ISBN: 978-1-5462-3449-4 (sc)
ISBN: 978-1-5462-3448-7 (e)

Library of Congress Control Number: 2018903662

Print information available on the last page.

For my dad; you are appreciated. You have taught me to be confident, and independent. You have always believed in me and supported me. You are my favorite mentor. I am honored and blessed to be your daughter. I hope I make you proud.

To my sister-Sonam; thank you for the encouragement and motivation. You are a pillar to my life, that holds everything together. Thank you for being my backbone. You are my role model and inspiration.

Mom; it's not easy to find the right words for you. Thank you is an immensely small phrase, for the sacrifices you have made. Thank you for teaching me what life really is. I hope that I can be half the person that you are today.

To Rajesh and Mudit; thank you for all the love, support and care. You both have always pushed me towards my goals and dreams.

My World Turned Around

When you came into my life,
My world turned around.
I felt as if I was being crowned.

With your love so powerful
And desire so colorful,
My soul was drowned.

When you came into my life,
My world turned around.

With a smile so beautiful
And eyes blissful,
My strength was found.

When you came into my life,
My world turned around.

The Way We Met

The way we met,
With our lips so wet.

The eyes like wine,
Which makes you mine.

The way we met,
With our lips so wet.

A soul with wild desire,
Which makes my smile fire.

The way we met,
With our lips so wet.

Let Us Wander

Let us wander
Along the roadside.

Take my hand,
And twirl a magic wand.

We will make an escape
With our bodies covered in drapes.

Let us wander
Along the roadside.

With heavily pouring rain,
My love for you will not go in vain.

My Words

I use my words,
And they set me free.

They are infused deep inside,
With tears that are dried.

Sometimes in agony they suffer.
Fearing from the dark,
They leave a spark.

Hiding everything you cannot hear
With the mask that my smile wears.

I use my words,
And they set me free.

Every Month

Every month
This day becomes more and more special for me.
I wish to get down on my knees.

We have created a beautiful bond,
With our love so beyond.

You have always made me feel so alive,
Handling my emotional outbursts
By putting my priorities first.

You treat me like a queen
With your heart so clean.

Thank you for being there
And for all the love and care.

Wish

All I wish is to see you
With our love so true.

Your smile,
Your laugh
Make me go all blue.

A wedding with you is planned
With our pictures scanned.

We will conquer the world
With our hearts pearled.

Nobody Knows

Nobody knows
The screams,
The cries,
The sobbing.

Nobody knows
The empty smile.

Nobody knows
It's painful.

They think I am strong,
But I feel trapped
In chains.

Time

It's about time that I face it now.
I have been waiting forever
To realise that we are not together.

Nothing can stop the time.
Being apart from you feels like a crime.

When will the suffering stop?
My sentiments seem to be chopped.

My heart needs to know
That nothing lasts forever,
But my love for you will never end.

Far Away

So far away
But so close.
Haven't met you yet,
But my thoughts are set.

Don't know if our destinies will ever intertwine,
Though my heart gives me a sign.

Insecurities

Scars,
Stretch marks,
Cuts,
Wounds.

As much as she tried,
She failed.

Her mind kept wandering like a hurricane,
Sometimes with thoughts,
Sometimes with pain.

She wanted to get out of the cage,
But her life never turned the page.

Scars,
Stretch marks,
Cuts,
Wounds.

As much as she tried,
She failed.

Pain

It's demanding.
It needs her.

The pain!
Why?

Why can't it be alone?
Why does it need company?

It wants the eyes,
The cries,
It wants the wrists,
The cuts.

Bitterness

Hot,
Without sugar,
Some cream,
Coffee.

Now I understand.

Bitter,
Cruel love.

Yet
I have it every day.

It will get better with time.

Hot,
One sugar,
Some cream,
Coffee.

Love Battle

It's hard to define
The way I adored you.
It's not just that.
You had no clue.

You said you loved me.
Deep inside I knew
That wasn't true.

I woke up from the dream
Feeling the defeat,
Knowing the battle wasn't worth it,
And my destiny would cheat.

Cage

Every day I start with a blank page,
Hoping to write something to help others.
But in return, it eases my pain,
And I end up in a cage.

As the heartfelt phrases are formed,
Tears rush down my cheeks
And formation of sadness seeks.

Help

It's time again,
When frustration crawls up my mind;
Misery surrounds my soul.

I endure to be restless,
Helpless.
I need help in ways I don't understand.

As I stand still,
Thoughts after thoughts,
Chills after chills.

Now I must surrender,
With hopes to walk again.

Heaviness

"Letting go is easy," is what they say.
They don't know
How much my heart weighs.

I lied to everyone,
Saying, "I am fine,"
Making myself believe
You are mine.

I heard the whispers,
The laughs
And giggles.

I wished this wouldn't end
Because our love was a new trend.

Now I am grateful
That my heart was shattered
As he came
To put all the pieces together.
And that's all that matters.

Drifted

Something is fading between us.
There are things that need to be discussed.

We are drifting apart
With changes in our hearts.

Something is wrong;
Our bond was strong.

It seems to be unfair
With a different air.

Fear

Fear,
Tears,
Happen every day.
Life seems to be gray.

I want to run away
And make a sweet escape.

I say I am fine,
Thinking what the time will bring,
But my day can never shine.

Fear,
Tears,
Happen every day.
Life seems to be gray.

Unexpected

Unexpected,
The day was here.
He was standing in front of her,
Ready to mend her world.

Clock stopped ticking
As she stood still,
Shivering.

He wanted to fix the broken,
But rudeness was her loudest cry.

She was scared
To fade again,
So she took a step back
And pushed him away.

Rain

I fell apart
As you left me
In the rain,
Without turning back.

Droplets dripping down,
Pounding in sorrow,
With no difference in tears and rain.

As I wiped away my tears,
Looked ahead,
Balanced myself,
And made my way home.

That moment destroyed my serenity,
Causing my heart to ache.

Torn

Torn,
Burned
Like a piece of paper.

There was no end to this;
I had to accept it.

It became hard to decide.
Was I weak or strong?
And where did I belong?

Visualizing my past,
The chaotic pain,
My body felt numb.

Torn,
Burned
Like a piece of paper.

One Day

Longing for one day
To chase my dreams,
But I fail to make my way.

I feel like drowning
In my own anger,
With my heart desperately shouting.

Wanting my anger to melt
As I walk down the darkness,
Wearing my stilettos as a weapon,
Accepting the reality.

Demons

As if
Each line was rehearsed.

"I will not leave you," was what he said.
I convinced myself to give him a chance.

Yet
At a single glance,
I was left alone
To face the demons.

Demons that terrified me,
Made me vulnerable.

Seemed like I was thrown down the cliff,
Realizing everyone is at the same level,
Just with different devils.

Reflection

Every day
I sit next to the fireplace
With a pen and paper in hand.

As I notice my own glimmering reflection,
With the thirst to see perfection.

Missing my laughter and smile,
My body tremors in disguise.

I put my head down in disappointment
And begin to write again.

Expectations

I wanted him to catch a glimpse
of my tears.

I wanted to immerse my broken soul
gently in his hands.

I wanted him to sense
my misery.

I wanted him to understand me
a little better.

Or was I expecting
too much?

At the end he would leave
Was what I thought.

To fight the demons again.

Printed in the United States
By Bookmasters